12/03

In all the world,
my dearest friend, there is
no better gift than you.

To My dearest
friend
Love
from
Marsie

Thank You, Friend

new seasons™

Contributing writers: Rebecca Christian, Marie Jones,
Jennifer John Ouellette, Lynda Twardowski

Picture credits: © **Corbis:** Christie's Images; Images.com;
Swim Ink; **SuperStock:** Bridgeman Art Library, London; Christie's Images;
Lauros-Giraudon, Paris; Charles Neal;
Sorolla Museum, Valencia, Spain

New Seasons is a trademark of Publications International, Ltd.

Louis Weber, CEO
Publications International, Ltd.
7373 N. Cicero Avenue
Lincolnwood, Illinois 60712

www.pilbooks.com

Manufactured in China.

8 7 6 5 4 3 2 1

ISBN: 1-4127-0618-1

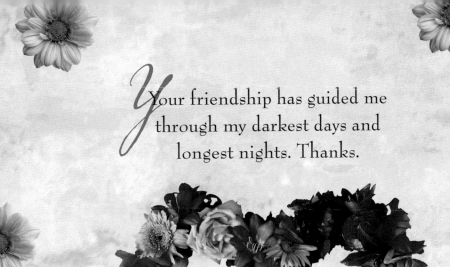

Your friendship has guided me through my darkest days and longest nights. Thanks.

Counting the reasons I appreciate you is like counting leaves on a tree… I lose my place long before I finish.

$\mathcal{T}$hank you for believing in me and for encouraging me to go after the life of my dreams. I hope you will always be a part of it.

Thank you for helping me see life's little embarrassing moments as material for a comedy routine instead of traumatizing incidents that require years of therapy.

Thanks for being that special kind of friend who knows exactly when to be honest and when it's best to tell me what I want and need to hear!

Sometimes I ride high, sometimes I sink low.
Your friendship is the elastic that
snaps me back to center.

Great friends like you are hard to find, harder to hang on to, and hardest still to let go of. That's why I'm holding on to you for dear life. You are a priceless treasure.

Thank you for understanding
that when I have a problem,
I don't want a solution, advice,
or even sympathy—I just need
someone to listen.

You are my lighthouse in a storm. You guide me through treacherous seas and light the way for my voyage home.

A friend is someone who is honest enough to warn you when you are about to make a big mistake and kind enough not to tease you when you make it anyway.

Isn't it funny how two such ordinary people can find in each other such extraordinary friendship?

Thank you for those times you've gently told me I might want to look at something another way. Your tact and honesty make your advice worth listening to.

*I*f I could reach the stars,
I'd bring one down to illuminate
your thoughtfulness.

People aren't as loyal as they used to be.
And that's just another reason I'm
grateful for you.

When I'm down, you pick me up.
When I'm scared, you back me up.
And when I cry, you crack me up.
What more could I need in a friend?

A friend makes life so much sweeter.
Thank you for sweetening my life.
A friend makes life so much brighter.
Thank you for brightening my life.

Many people are sunny skies and good times friends. A few people are rainy times and catastrophe friends. Thanks for being both. I can always count on you.

When we're together,
it doesn't matter if the
skies pour or the winds
howl or all of our plans go
awry. You have a rare
ability to transform a
disaster into an adventure.

*Y*our friendship gives
me the courage to be
what I want to be.

You're not just my friend but my teacher. I'm grateful for the way you've taught me to listen attentively, to offer a shoulder in good times and bad, to love unconditionally. You've taught me how to be a friend.

True friends like you are as rare as triple rainbows and as precious as rubies and emeralds by the ton. True friends like you are a treasure that cannot be measured.

Friendship is a
seed planted
during a chance
first meeting that
grows into a flower
when it's watered
with love. Thank
you for tending
our garden of
friendship.

When I don't
have strength,
I have you, my friend.
And that has made
all the difference.

If laughter is the best medicine, our friendship should be the No. 1 doctor-prescribed remedy.

We may not be related by blood or share a last name, but we are closely connected where it counts—in heart and in spirit. I cherish you, friend.

I like to go shopping
with you because you
have never let me
commit a fashion
faux pas just to be nice.

*I*f I'm grumpy... you sit beside me with your arms
    crossed, too.
If I'm sad... you share my tears.
If I need comfort... you open your arms.
If I'm ecstatic and want to yell it from the
    mountains... you echo my voice across the valley.
That's what I'm most thankful for. I never have to
    explain myself—I just have to be me.

*I*f I am a good friend
to you it is because
I learned from
your example.

My buddy, my crony, my pal, my partner in crime. I thank you for all you are to me.

Thank you, friend, for being the anchor amidst the stormy seas of my life. Only a real friend like you could put up with my tendency for drama!

Having a friend like you is like sweet rain upon a parched field in the dead of summer. So please humor me if I shower you with love, affection, and gratitude.

*I*sn't it amazing that we have no blood or family ties? Fate just crossed our paths and tied our hearts forever in a friendship knot.

I have many friends
but only one that I
would call treasured
and true, and that,
my friend, is you.
For all the ways you
make my life more
meaningful and
happy, I thank you
from the bottom of
my heart.

When the world shuts its doors and locks me out, you are the key that welcomes me back in.

Thank you for never trying to give me advice when you knew what I really wanted was someone to listen. Only a dear friend like you could be so kind, intuitive, and patient.

I'll never forget that time
I fell off my diet and into
a hot fudge sundae. You
said the right thing:
"Whipped cream doesn't
have any carbohydrates."

*T*he best thing about having you for a friend is the way you never fail to make me see the silver lining behind each dark cloud. No matter how down I get, I can always count on you to help me find a reason to get back up and try again.

A true friend is someone who still thinks you are pretty cool even when you are acting like the biggest nerd on earth. Thanks for having the heart to spare my feelings!

Thank you, dear friend, for making the bumps along my life path a little less rocky. You smooth over the rough edges of my days with your love, support, and laughter.

Thank you for teaching me how to be the
kind of friend worth having.

I don't mind my wrinkles much; they come courtesy of the many years I spent laughing with you.

Your friendship has been the best medicine: my soothing balm when I am anxious or afraid, my elixir when I am feeling out of sorts.
You are a healing force in my life.

Thank you for being that
special kind of friend
who always manages to
stay close at heart, even
when you can't always be
close at hand.

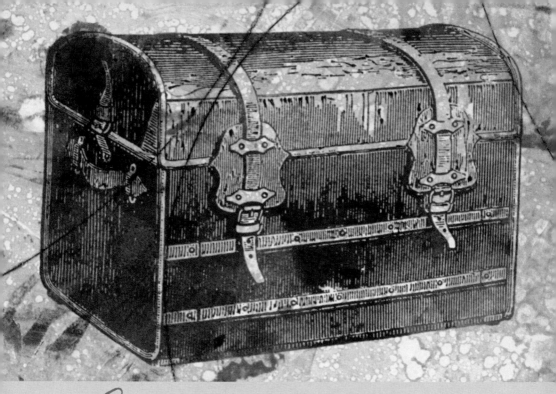

A friend like you is worth more to me than all the money, jewels, and riches in the world. Your friendship makes me feel like a million dollars, and that's all the wealth I need!

Knowing you're always behind me is often my best reason for moving forward.

You are the only one who can make me giggle through my tears and make me laugh until I cry.

Time may heal all wounds, but it is
our friends who give us the strength
to endure each hour in between.
Thanks for giving me strength.

What you have given me is so much more than just friendship. You have given me a reason to sing, to smile, to dance, to laugh, and to grow.

Our friendship is
like super-strength
glue: We have an
impenetrable bond.
I'm sticking
to you for life!

The best way I know
to say thank you for
your wonderful
friendship is to try to
be the kind of friend
to you that you have
always been to me.

Friendship isn't a gift you hold in your hands but a blessing you carry in your heart.

*Y*ou are so much more than just my friend. You are a traveling companion on the path of life, sharing laughter, hopes, and dreams as we walk side by side.

*Y*ou are a firefly in the night. You light the darkness and bring amazement and awe to everyone around you.

Our best friends aren't counted on our fingers; they are simply counted on.

For always making time, never telling lies, and
faithfully being my support...thank you.

Good friends know all your old jokes; great friends still laugh at them.

What I love so much about visiting you is that somehow you always make me feel that I am the one person in the world you most wanted to see.

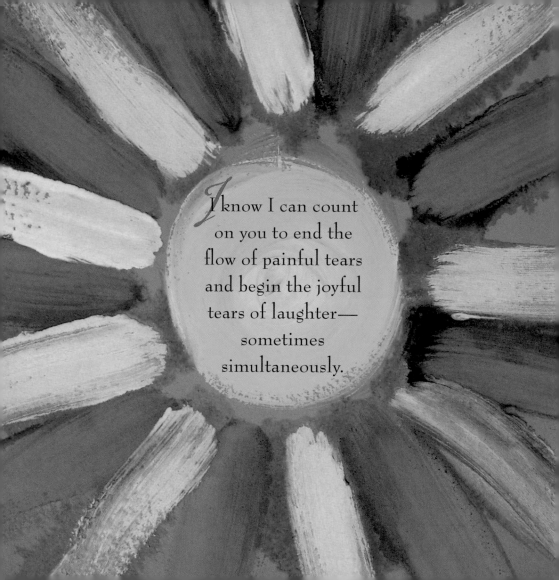

I know I can count on you to end the flow of painful tears and begin the joyful tears of laughter— sometimes simultaneously.

Through heartaches and joys, downfalls
and triumphs, victories and failures,
we've always been there to cheer each
other on or cheer each other up. I am so
blessed to call you my friend.

*I*f I lost my hair, lost my teeth, and lost my mind, I could go on, so long as I don't lose you, my friend.

What I most appreciate about you is that you tell me what I need to hear even though you know I'd rather hear something else! You have the courage to be honest with me.

You are a beacon of light.
Thank you for shining your
friendship on my life.

Good friends open their heart and lend their ear; true friends open their closet and lend their clothes.

We've seen it all, tried it all, and even done it all. I thank my lucky stars that we've been through it all together.

What is a dear friend but someone
to share in the joyful rhythm of life?
Thank you for being half of this
amazing friendship.

My prized possession in all the world
    is nothing that can be held or shown—
it is the friendship that over the years
    the two of us have nurtured and grown.

My life was good before we met, but now that you are my friend, life is so much better than good, it's great!

What good is life if you don't have somebody special to share each and every moment of it with? I love you for always being there, for every up and every down and everything in between.

Thank you, my friend, for the love you never fail to offer, the help you never fail to give, and the laughter you never cease to share. Without you, my life would be half empty. With you, I feel happy, whole, and complete.

There is nothing in this world that I can't handle
when I have you behind me in support.

Best friends make the best dinner dates. You can spill your wine, spill your guts, and still expect a call tomorrow. Thanks for always being there.

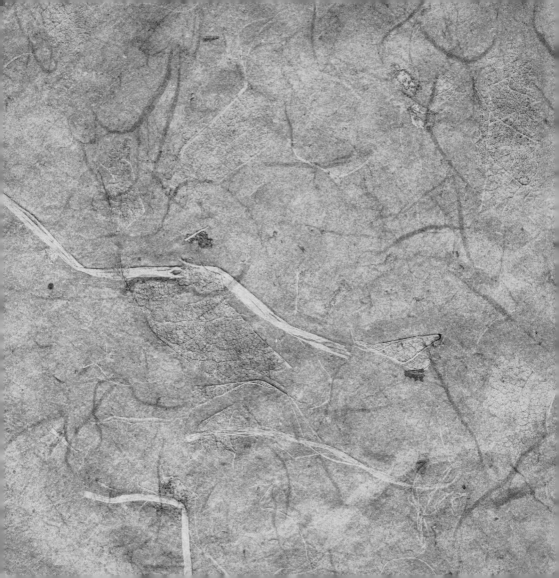